Think Like a Scientist

Written by Melissa Blackwell Burke

T 41722

STECK-VAUGHN
ELEMENTARY · SECONDARY · ADULT · LIBRARY

A Harcourt Classroom Education Company

www.steck-vaughn.com

Contents

Chapter 1

Think Like a

What would you like to learn about the world? What problem would you like to solve? These are things scientists often think about. They consider what the answer might be. Then they set out to find the answer. As they work, scientists think about what they see. They think about what has happened in the past. They think about why things seem surprising. Much of a scientist's job is thinking.

Scientists work in many different fields of science from **astronomy** to **physics**. This book introduces you to six interesting fields of science. It also invites you to "be" each type of scientist. So, as you learn about scientists and their work, get ready to think like a scientist!

Scientists study many things in each field of science. Some scientists study diseases. Other scientists study soil. Whatever scientists are studying, they spend much time thinking.

Scientists follow a special way, or order, of doing things. They use the **scientific method** to guide their thinking. The scientific method begins with a question. Then scientists make a **hypothesis**, or guess, about the answer. To test their guess, they **experiment**. Then they study the **results**. Scientists may do an experiment many times to study the results. As you do the experiments in this book, think like a scientist.

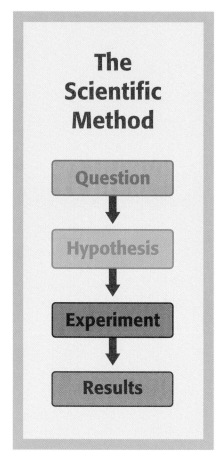

The Scientific Method

Question

Hypothesis

Experiment

Results

As scientists work, they also think about being safe. They use many safety rules to protect themselves and others. The experiments discussed in this book have safety rules, too. The safety rules are here to keep you safe as you do experiments and think like a scientist.

SAFETY

for Young Scientists

⚠ Get adult help when working with anything hot, sharp, or poisonous.

⚠ Wear goggles or safety glasses when working with **chemicals**.

⚠ Ask an adult whether things are safe to touch.

⚠ Wash all bottles, jars, and other containers before and after using.

⚠ Keep the work area tidy.

 Some chemicals don't mix safely. Ask an adult before you stir things!

Chapter 2

Think Like an

Astronomer

People have wondered about space since early times. What is out there? How can stars, comets, and even the rising and setting of the sun be explained?

Scientists who study space are **astronomers**. They observe the sun, stars, and comets. They also study planets, moons, and how light travels. Astronomy is the study of all things in outer space.

Astronomers constantly make new discoveries. Using telescopes that make distant objects appear closer, astronomers find things no one knew were in space, such as far-away stars and dust clouds. Now new, more powerful telescopes are being built, which allow astronomers to see farther into space than ever before.

You might picture astronomers working at night, gazing up at the stars. In fact, most astronomers spend few nights a year at a telescope. They spend many days at a computer studying and tracking data. Some astronomers get information from **satellites** orbiting in

Huge telescopes help astronomers see planets and stars in outer space.

space. Others plan space missions for astronauts.

Many astronomers study stars, how light travels from them, and the distance between them. The distance between stars is measured in **light-years**. A light-year is the distance that light travels in a year. Astronomers also study the brightness of stars. Have you ever wondered why stars seem to twinkle? To try and find out, do the experiment on the next page.

Why Do Stars Twinkle?

Materials
- aluminum foil (12-inch x 12-inch square)
- tap water
- 2-quart clear glass bowl
- flashlight

Experiment

1. Gently crumple the foil. Then spread it flat on a table.

2. Fill the glass bowl half full with water. Put it on top of the foil.

3. For best results, turn off the lights. Turn on the flashlight. Hold the flashlight about one foot above the bowl.

4. Tap the side of the bowl gently with your hand.

5. Observe how the foil looks through the water.

6. You may also wish to observe the light reflected from the bowl onto a low ceiling.

What did you find out? How did the foil look when you shined the light on it? What happened when the water began to move?

The experiment shows why stars seem to twinkle. In the experiment, the light rays from the flashlight bend as they move through the water. In space, light bends as it moves through different thicknesses of air.

Astronomers often try to find out how things happen in space. They study how stars are formed. They study how stars die. Astronomers try to solve the mysteries of the universe.

Light rays bend as they move through the air and water.

Chapter 3

Think Like a

What is the same about your body, paint, and a rubber ball? They are all made from chemicals.

Chemistry is the study of **matter**. Matter is anything that takes up space and has mass. **Chemists** are people who study what happens when two or more kinds of matter combine and react.

There are many special areas of chemistry. Some chemists work to create products or make them better. Some products are things we use every day, such as household cleansers, metals, plastics, and paint. Other chemists work to solve problems in the world, such as pollution. Another area of chemistry looks for cures for diseases.

Chemists wear safety goggles when they do experiments with chemicals.

Chemists work with chemicals to make many things. They may combine different chemicals to make medicines. They may combine different chemicals to make bug spray. Some chemists work to combine different chemicals to make perfume.

To think like a chemist, try doing the experiment on the next page. But before doing the experiment, be sure to talk to an adult. Learn all that you can about each of the chemicals you are mixing. There are some chemical combinations that are dangerous to your health.

What Happens
When Glue, Water, and Borax Mix?

Materials

- 1 teaspoon borax (found with laundry detergents in supermarkets)
- 1 cup distilled water
- spoon
- glass bowl or other container
- white school glue
- tap water
- paper towels
- safety goggles

Experiment

1. Put on safety goggles. Pour the distilled water and borax into the bowl. Stir. Let it stand for five minutes.

2. Stir the mixture. As you stir, squeeze a thin stream of glue into it. Keep stirring the mixture. Stop the glue when the spoon is covered.

3. Take the spoon out of the mixture. Use your hands to pull the white matter off the spoon. Wash the matter in cold tap water.

4. Dry your hands with the paper towels. Roll the matter in your hands to dry it. Shape it into a ball.

5. Drop the ball onto a table or floor.

What happened? How did the mixture look? How did it change?

The experiment shows how matter can react and change. Alone, glue can't bounce, but when combined with borax, it takes on a new shape.

That's what chemistry is all about. Chemists put different chemicals together to see how they will combine and react.

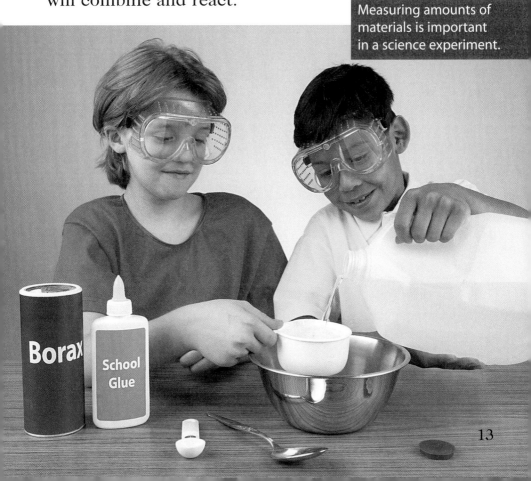

Measuring amounts of materials is important in a science experiment.

Chapter 4

Think Like a

Geologist

Think about the earth under your feet. Does it appear to be changing? It is. Deep inside the earth, rocks are moving and changing all the time. **Geology** is the study of Earth and its changes. Some **geologists** study past changes on Earth. That way, they can predict what might happen in the future.

Some geologists study huge changes on Earth, such as volcanic eruptions. By using information about past eruptions, they can tell when a volcano might erupt. Many geologists today are keeping an eye on a volcano in Mexico called "Popo." If they see changes they think mean an eruption is on the way, they will warn people to seek safety.

Geologists study changes below Earth's surface after a volcanic eruption.

Some geologists predict when and where earthquakes might happen. They study the movement of rock below the earth's surface. Geologists can tell whether the movement is an earthquake or not.

You can make an instrument similar to one that geologists use to measure earthquakes. To make one, try the experiment on the next page.

How Can Earthquakes Be Measured?

Materials
- 1 quart jar with lid
- felt-tip pen with wide point
- rubber band
- masking tape
- scissors
- wax paper
- ruler
- tap water

Experiment

1. Fill the jar half full with water. Close the lid.

2. Cut wax paper into a 6-inch by 12-inch strip. Lay it on a table. Set the jar at one end of the paper.

3. Remove the pen cap. Use the rubber band to strap the pen to the jar. Make sure the point is down. Let the pen's point touch the paper. Tape the pen to the jar.

4. Grab the free end of the paper.

5. Gently hold the jar with one hand.

6. Slowly pull the paper straight out from under the jar.

7. Observe the line on the paper.

8. Repeat the experiment while a partner gently shakes the table.

Did you record any movement? Was either line wavy? Was either line straight?

The experiment shows how one tool that geologists use works. A straight line with tiny waves indicates that the earth is moving but an earthquake is not happening. During an earthquake, a wavy, jumpy line is recorded.

Geologists study Earth's changes. They may study changes from millions of years ago that made resources such as gems and oil. Other geologists study changes that might be dangerous to people, such as earthquakes and volcanoes.

The pen is recording the movement of Earth.

Chapter 5

Think Like a Meteorologist

Have you ever wished you could change the weather? People can't do that, but they can predict what the weather will be. The science of weather is called **meteorology**. Studying and forecasting weather is the job of a **meteorologist**.

Have you seen a meteorologist on TV? Those news forecasts help people plan and prepare. But only about 1 out of 10 meteorologists appear on the news. Meteorologists study weather conditions and their causes. Meteorologists study the causes of extreme weather, such as tornadoes and floods. They study ways to change the weather, too. Meteorologists can also work on special projects. Some work to help stop air pollution. Others work with airlines to help make flying safe.

Meteorologists are constantly watching and studying weather because it occurs 24 hours a day. They issue weather warnings when needed. They track weather data. Meteorologists use the weather data to develop accurate weather forecasts. They also work around the clock to measure changing weather conditions.

Strong tornado winds can spin up to 300 miles per hour.

Some weather conditions are very severe. Tornadoes and hurricanes can hurt people. They cause damage to property. Some meteorologists follow tornadoes. Others track hurricanes.

To better understand a weather condition, meteorologists often observe what happens. Have you ever wondered how a tornado looks up close? To try and find out, do the experiment on the next page.

19

What Does a Tornado Look Like?

Materials
- medium to large flat-bottomed juice bottle with cap
- dishwashing liquid
- 8–10 marbles
- tap water

Experiment
1. Fill the bottle almost full with water.
2. Add one small drop of dishwashing liquid.
3. Put the marbles into the bottle. Close the cap tightly.
4. Hold the bottle sideways. Swirl it around and around so that the marbles spin.
5. Put the bottle down quickly and observe.

What did you see? How did the tornado look? How would you describe its movement?

This experiment shows the action of a tornado. The wind in a tornado spins in a cone-shape. At the same time, it spins upward.

Meteorologists work with equipment to watch a storm's path and speed. They use what they know about weather patterns to make a guess about what might happen.

People's lives can change in an instant because of weather. And weather can change quickly, too. That's why the weather forecast isn't always right. But weather forecasting helps people stay safe.

The water acts like the wind in a tornado.

Chapter 6

Think Like an

Oceanographer

Have you heard about projects to save whales or other ocean life that is in danger? Some **oceanographers** are in charge of those efforts. **Oceanography** is the study of oceans and their effects on Earth.

Oceans make Earth special. Oceanographers work to understand and explain oceans. They also try to solve ocean problems. One of the biggest problems for oceans is pollution. People dump garbage into ocean waters. Companies dump oil and other wastes into ocean waters. This pollution hurts the animals living there as well as the beauty of the water. Oceanographers work to protect the ocean waters and ocean life. Others work with the oil and gas companies to help find hidden resources on the floor of oceans. Still others teach about oceans.

To learn more about oceans and their effects on Earth, oceanographers spend a lot of time testing and observing ocean waters. One thing oceanographers study is how **currents** move around Earth. Currents are the paths in which water moves. Oceanographers study the temperature and the amount of salt in the water. They also study the shape of the ocean floor. Oceanographers work to discover secrets of the sea.

Have you ever wondered how water moves in the ocean? To try and find out, do the experiment on the next page.

Oceanographers use diving gear to breathe underwater.

How Does Water Temperature Affect Currents?

Materials
- blue and red food coloring
- two clear drinking glasses
- two clear measuring cups
- pitcher of cool tap water
- medicine dropper
- ice
- 1 quart jar
- pitcher of very hot tap water

Experiment
1. Fill the jar half full with ice. Add cool tap water to the top. Let it stand for five minutes.

2. Fill one measuring cup one-quarter full with cold water from the jar. Label the cup *cold*.

3. Add blue food coloring until the water is very dark blue.

4. Fill one glass with hot tap water. Fill the dropper with blue cold water.

5. Put the dropper into the hot water and squeeze very slowly. Watch the movement of the blue water.

6. Fill the other glass with cold water from the jar.

7. Repeat steps 2–5 with a few changes. Use hot water in step 2. Use red food coloring in step 3. Fill the dropper with red, hot water in step 4. Put the dropper into the cold water and squeeze in step 5. Watch the movement of the red water.

What did you see? How did the temperature of the water affect the movement? How would this affect a current in the ocean?

In the experiment, you saw that temperature affects how water moves. This is the same thing that happens in the ocean.

Oceanographers study the patterns of ocean flow or currents. These patterns can affect the weather. They affect the paths ships travel. The patterns of ocean flow also affect the lives of ocean animals.

Cold water and hot water move at different speeds.

Chapter 7

Think Like a

Physicist

Maybe you have flown in an airplane. Perhaps you've had an x-ray taken. Have you ever used electricity? If you've done any of these, you have dealt with physics. Physics is the study of forces. **Physicists** work with ideas about motion, light, and energy.

Physicists look for rules or laws that explain why things move the way they do. The same laws can help explain the movement of a ball thrown in the air or a planet in space.

Physicists often work on the cutting edge of technology. For example, they use very powerful computers as they work. They may also work with high-powered lasers. They may work with all types of engines.

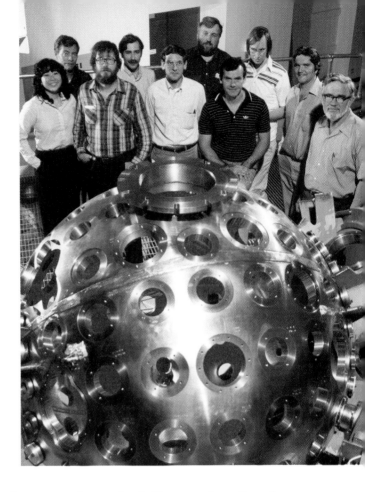

Physicists use high-energy lasers in their work.

Physicists often work with different kinds of energy. They study energy to see how it is produced, how it travels, and how it can be used.

Physicists also study magnets and electricity. Sometimes electricity is flowing. Other times it is not flowing, and it is called static electricity. To try and find out more about static electricity, do the experiment on the next page.

What Is the Effect of Static Electricity?

Materials
- 1/4 cup crisped rice cereal
- plate of Plexiglas, about 12 inches x 12 inches
- 4 small wooden blocks
- wool object, such as a sweater

Experiment

1. Place 4 small wooden blocks in a rectangular shape on a table.

2. Pour 1/4 cup of cereal inside the block-shaped area.

3. Gently spread out the cereal.

4. Rub the Plexiglas on both sides with the wool object. Rub it hard.

5. Place the Plexiglas on top of the blocks.

6. Watch the cereal.

What happened? Why do you think the cereal moved as it did?

In the experiment, you created a static charge. This happened when you rubbed the wool object onto the plate. The pieces of cereal had an opposite charge from the plate. The unlike charges attracted. This made the cereal move. When the charge fades away, the cereal falls down.

Studying charges and electricity is part of physics. And electricity is an important part of everyday life.

Static electricity causes the cereal to cling to the plate.

More to Explore

Use this chart to find titles of books and software about astronomy, chemistry, geology, meteorology, oceanography, and physics.

Astronomy

Astronomy (Pocket Facts) by Philip Steele

Discovering the Planets by Jacqueline Mitton

Be Your Own Astronomy Expert by Gillaime Cannat, Nathalie Locoste, Jean-Claude Senee

Interactive Science Encyclopedia CD-ROM *(Steck-Vaughn Company)*

Chemistry

Eyewitness Science: Chemistry by Ann Newmark

Chemistry (Science Projects) by Chris Fairclough

It's Elementary: Investigating the Chemical World by Douglas Hayward and Gordon Bates

Interactive Science Encyclopedia CD-ROM *(Steck-Vaughn Company)*

Geology

Exploring the World of Geology by George Burns

Strange Science: Planet Earth by Bernice Mascher

Earth: Forces and Formations CD-ROM *(Steck-Vaughn Company)*

Message in a Fossil: Uncovering the Past® CD-ROM *(Steck-Vaughn Company)*

Violent Earth CD-ROM *(Steck-Vaughn Co.)*

Meteorology

Hurricanes and Tornadoes by Neil Morris

Weather by Tony Potter and Martin Lunn

Weather (Nature Detective) by Anita Ganeri and Mike Atkinson

Weather, Climate, and You!™ CD-ROM *(Steck-Vaughn Company)*

Our Environment CD-ROM *(Steck-Vaughn Company)*

Oceanography

The Pacific Ocean by David Lambert

Beneath the Oceans by Penny Clarke

The Mysterious Ocean Highway: Benjamin Franklin and the Gulf Stream by Deborah Heiligman

Interactive Science Encyclopedia CD-ROM *(Steck-Vaughn Company)*

Our Environment CD-ROM *(Steck-Vaughn Company)*

www.turnstonepub.com

Physics

101 Physics Tricks: Fun Experiments With Everyday Materials by Terry Cash

Everyday Science by Michael H. Gabb

Forces and Motion by Simon De Pinna

Interactive Science Encyclopedia CD-ROM *(Steck-Vaughn Company)*

Glossary

astronomy/astronomer the study of outer space; the name of such a scientist

chemical a substance produced by or used in chemistry

chemistry/chemist the study of matter and how it reacts; the name of such a scientist

current a path in which water moves

experiment a test to discover or prove something

geology/geologist the study of the earth and its changes; the name of such a scientist

hypothesis a logical, scientific guess

light-year distance that light travels in a year

matter anything that takes up space and has mass

meteorology/meteorologist the study of weather; the name of such a scientist

oceanography/oceanographer the study of oceans; the name of such a scientist

physics/physicist the study of forces; the name of such a scientist

result the outcome of an experiment or action

satellite an object in space that orbits around another larger object

scientific method a way of solving problems: ask a question, form a hypothesis, experiment, and study the results

Index